A BARD UNKEND:
*Selected Poems
in the Scottish Dialect*

by

GAVIN TURNBULL

Scottish Poetry Reprints Series
An occasional series edited by G. Ross Roy, 1970-1996

1. *The Life and Death of the Piper of Kilbarchan*, by Robert Semphill, edited by G. Ross Roy (Edinburgh: Tragara Press, 1970).
2. *Peblis, to the Play*, edited by A. M. Kinghorn (London: Quarto Press, 1974).
3. *Archibald Cameron's Lament*, edited by G. Ross Roy (London: Quarto Press, 1977).
4. *Tam o' Shanter, A Tale*, by Robert Burns, edited by G. Ross Roy from the Afton Manuscript (London: Quarto Press, 1979).
5. *Auld Lang Syne*, by Robert Burns, edited by G. Ross Roy, music transcriptions by Laurel E. Thompson and Jonathan D. Ensiminger (Greenock: Black Pennell Press, 1984).
6. *The Origin of Species*, by Lord Neaves, edited by Patrick Scott (London: Quarto Press, 1986).
7. *Robert Burns, A Poem*, by Iain Crichton Smith (Edinburgh: Morning Star, 1996).

***

8. *The Prayer of Holy Willie, A canting, hypocritical, Kirk Elder*, by Robert Burns; the Kilmarnock chapbook of 1789, edited by Patrick Scott (Columbia: Scottish Poetry Reprints, 2015).
9. *Tollerators and Con-Tollerators, a comedy*, attributed to Archibald Pitcairne, edited by John MacQueen (Columbia: Scottish Poetry Reprints, 2015).
10. *A Bard Unkend: Selected Poems in the Scottish Dialect*, by Gavin Turnbull, edited by Patrick Scott (Columbia: Scottish Poetry Reprints, 2015).

A Bard Unkend:
Selected Poems in the Scottish Dialect

by

Gavin Turnbull

edited and introduced by
Patrick Scott

Scottish Poetry Reprints
University of South Carolina Libraries
2015

Initial costs for the print version
of this Scottish Poetry Reprint
have been made possible through private donations.

Introduction © Patrick Scott, 2015.

All rights reserved.

Cover image courtesy of University of South Carolina Libraries.

This reprint is published through CreateSpace, and is available from CreateSpace, Amazon, and AmazonUK. It is not available for purchase direct from the University Libraries.

Editorial address:
Patrick Scott, c/o Irvin Department of Rare Books & Special Collections,
University of South Carolina Libraries,
1322 Greene Street, Columbia, SC 29208, U.S.A.

ISBN-13: 978-1514348512
ISBN-10: 1514348519

INTRODUCTION

> Dear Sir, if my unnotic'd name,
> Not yet proclaim'd by trump of fame,
> Has reach'd your lugs, then swith attend,
> This essay of a Bard unkend.
>   Turnbull, "Epistle to a Black-smith" (1788).

This selection draws attention to a neglected aspect of a largely-neglected Scottish poet, marking the 250th anniversary of his birth. Gavin Turnbull (1765-1816), a younger contemporary of Robert Burns, published two books of poetry in Scotland before he emigrated to America in 1795, and he continued to publish after he emigrated. What recent critical discussion there has been of Turnbull's poetry has largely focused on his writing in the pastoral, Spenserian style favoured by such earlier eighteenth-century Scots as James Thomson and James Beattie. But throughout his career, Turnbull also wrote lively, more conversational verse using the Scots vernacular, drawing from the poetic tradition associated with Allan Ramsay, Robert Fergusson, and Robert Burns himself.

    Gavin Turnbull was born in Berwickshire and brought up in Hawick.[1] He left school young and began writing poetry as a teenager in

---

[1] Information on Turnbull's early life is sketchy. The birth date given above is calculated from the 1813 naturalization record, which gives his age and also place of birth: see Brent Holcomb, *South Carolina Naturalizations* (Baltimore: Genealogical Publishing, 1985). See also David Hill Radcliffe, "Turnbull, Gavin (c. 1765-1816)," *Oxford Dictionary of National Biography*, ed. H. C. G. Matthew and Brian Harrison (Oxford: Oxford UP, 2004), 55: 587, and Patrick Scott, "Whatever Happened to Gavin Turnbull? Hunting Down a Friend of Burns in South Carolina," *Robert Burns Lives!*, ed. Frank Shaw, no. 159 (November 28, 2012), at: http://www.electricscotland.com/familytree/frank/burns_lives159.htm.

Kilmarnock, where he was working as a carpet-weaver. The fullest description of his life at this time speaks both of hardship and literary commitment:

> He resided alone in a small garret, ... in which there was no furniture. The bed on which he lay was entirely composed of straw, ... with the exception of an old patched covering which he threw over himself at night. He had no chair to sit upon. A cold stone placed by the fire; and the sole of a small window at one end of the room was all he had for a table, from which to take his food, or on which to write his verses.[2]

This account fits with Turnbull's rueful self-portrait in his "Epistle to a Taylor" as being:

> A poet, tatter'd and forlorn,
> Whase coat and breeks are sadly torn. ...
> A ragged Bard, however gabby,
> Will ay be counted dull and shabby;

It fits too with his "Ode to David Sillar," though there he sees his deprivation less bleakly:

> Then heed na, Davie, tho' we be
> A race expos'd to misery,
>   A' mankind hae their skair;
> Yet, wi' the few whase hearts are fir'd
> Wi' love o' sang, by Him inspir'd,
>   What mortals can compare.

By the time he was twenty-three Turnbull had written enough poetry to fill a very substantial volume. Most of the poems in his *Poetical Essays* are in the Augustan pastoral style, often quite conventional lyrics on the themes of love and nature, using classical names for the "shepherds" who must stand in for the young Kilmarnock carpet-weaver:

> Muse, sing the passion of a rural pair,
> Damon the swain, Amanda was the fair:
> Long time he burn'd with love's resistless fire,
> And she as long, conceal'd the same desire;
>   (*Poetical Essays*, p. 84).

Even his poem of tribute to Robert Burns, "The Bard," uses the Spenserian stanza and antique Spenserian vocabulary:

> There whilom ligd, ypent in garret high,
> A tuneful Bard, who well could touch the lyre,
> Who often sung so soot, and witchingly

---

[2] Thomas Crichton, in *The Weaver*, 2 (Paisley, 1819), quoted in James Paterson, *The Contemporaries of Burns* (Edinburgh: Paton, 1840), 93.

As made the crowds, in silent gaze, admire,
Ymolten with the wild seraphic fire ... [3]

The epigraphs to and allusions in the poems suggest a range of reading, perhaps from anthologies or selections, comparable to that of Burns: Spenser, Milton, Shakespeare, Dryden, Pope, Thomson, Shenstone, Gray. It was this pastoral poetry that Turnbull himself put first when arranging the contents of his first book.

Yet the same years when Turnbull was writing away in his Kilmarnock garret saw the appearance of Robert Burns's first book, *Poems Chiefly in the Scottish Dialect* (1786). As a young man in Kilmarnock, Turnbull knew Burns (Burns would later write of him as "an old friend of mine"), and he was acquainted with other writers from Burns's circle. Turnbull was also familar with Scots poetry; there are epigraphs from or allusions to Ramsay, Hamilton of Bangour, Fergusson, James Graeme, and Michael Bruce, and Turnbull wrote tributes then or later not only to Burns himself, but to Ramsay and Fergusson.

It should be no surprise, therefore, that some three-quarters through *Poetical Essays* Turnbull included a section boldly titled *Poetical Essays in the Scottish Dialect*. The "dialect" is often fairly light, requiring little annotation, but the poems cover a spectrum of topics as also of vernacular styles. "The Cottage," a paean to rural independence in Spenserian metre that looks back to Fegusson's "Farmer's Ingle" and Burns's "The Cotter's Saturday Night," starts formally and its Scots becomes more evident as the reader is taken into the farmstead and then inside the cottage itself:

A twa-arm'd chair within the neuk ye'll see,
Where aft the guidman leans, wi' meikle glee,
And smoaks his pipe, and tells his pawky tale,
An antic ambry, made of aiken tree,
Wi' caps and luggies, rang'd upon a dale,
And meikle toop-horn spoons, and plates to haud the kail.

"Sale of Stationary Ware," about a Kilmarnock bookshop, using, the Standard Habbie or "Burns stanza," cannot be scanned unless it is read as Scots:

"To a the Warle be it kend,"
That I by Auction do intend

---

[3] On this aspect of Turnbull's poetry, see David Hill Radcliffe's large-scale digital project, *Spenser and the Tradition: English Poetry, 1579-1830*, on line at: http://spenserians.cath.vt.edu/AuthorRecord.php?&action=GET&recordid=33336&page=AuthorRecord.

>   Great routh o' Goods and Geer to vend,
>   At lowest price;

Such poems as Turnbull's "Ode" to Burns's friend and fellow-poet David Sillar, or his "Epistle" to an otherwise-unknown Ayr blacksmith-poet, are friendly and conversational in a way Turnbull's English pastorals are not. The "Elegy on a Famous Philosopher," about John Goldie to whom Burns also paid tribute, uses the Burns stanza in a way that is affectionate and direct, but certainly not uncritical. And there is also a drinking song, "Ye lads that are plaguet wi' lasses," that is confident enough in its vernacular to incorporate the Latinate "memorandum," rather as Burns used the Latinate "variorum" in *The Jolly Beggars*. Turnbull is not Robert Burns, but these poems are readable, and attractive, and well worth critical attention.

It is not clear quite when Turnbull left Kilmarnock. His preface to *Poetical Essays*, dated "Glasgow Oct. 24th, 1788," says that "unfavourable circumstances in his situation" had hastened both his own departure and the last stages in printing the book.[4] In May 1789, Burns was enquiring as to Turnbull's whereabouts so he could forward some of the subscription money.[5] But in the early 1790s Turnbull went on to establish himself as an actor with the new theatre in Dumfries, with J. B. Williamson and Louisa Fontenelle. He wrote theatrical prologues and songs, and even a one-act comedy *The Recruit*, and he reconnected with Burns, who in October 1793 forwarded some of Turnbull's (English) songs to George Thomson for possible inclusion in his *Select Collection*

---

[4] By 1788, the market in Kilmarnock for local poetry seeking subscriptions must have been discouraging: while Burns had been successful, the other Kilmarnock poets, John Lapraik and David Sillar, both lost heavily. The ornaments on the section titles in *Poetical Essays* were also used in Burns's *Poems Chiefly in the Scottish Dialect* and several other books printed by John Wilson of Kilmarnock between 1786 and 1790 (see Scott, *Scottish Literary Review*, 7:1 [2015], 8-19), and this suggests that the bulk of the book may have been set and printed in Kilmarnock before Turnbull's flitting. Turnbull's *Poetical Essays* was the only book of poems to appear with the Niven imprint in the 1780s. Ornaments are not necessarily unique to a single printer, but city booksellers or printers often outsourced book work to printers in smaller towns. Niven only started printing work in 1785-86, and I have found these ornaments in only two of Niven's other publications in the relevant period, both from 1787: Geoffrey Mccalman's *Treatise on Tea*, and Thomas Dyche, *A Guide to the English Tongue*.

[5] G. Ross Roy, ed., *Letters of Robert Burns*, 2 vols. (Oxford: Clarendon Press, 1985), I: 399, 413-414.

of Original Scotish Airs.[6] He collected some of this new writing, including his play, and reprinted a few earlier items, as a second, smaller book, *Poems,* by Gavin Turnbull, Comedian (Dumfries: for the Author, 1794).

The most significant vernacular piece in the new volume was his prologue to Allan Ramsay's *The Gentle Shepherd,* in which Ramsay reports on his reception among the immortals:

> When Death, that camsheugh carl, had fell'd me,
> And first Elysian fouk beheld me,
> My auld blue bonnet on my head,
> And hamely Caledonian weed;
> They cry'd, "preserve's: what's yon droll body,
> That gangs just like a niddy noddy?
> 'Tis some bit poor auld Scottish herd":
> "Na faith!" quo' Hermes, "he's a Bard,
> Sic as the deel a' mae ye'll find,
> And ane of the Dramatic kind."
> Syne he pronounc'd aloud my name,
> A current passport for my fame. ...
> And a' that had a spunk of grace
> Gied me kind welcome to the place;

Turnbull's Dumfries poems also reflect the changing political climate in 1790s Scotland, with the government crackdown against any hint of sedition. The Dumfries theatre itself became the subject of conservative suspicion. In Dumfries, in late 1792, the audience in the pit sang the French revolutionary song "Ça ira," while hissing "God save the King," and when the Dumfries actors, including Turnbull, toured across the border to Whitehaven in March 1794, the Earl of Lonsdale had them arrested as vagrants, after they put on the insurrectionary Ossianic melodrama *Oscar and Malvina.* (Burnsians will recall this event from the fragment "Esopus to Maria"). In 1794, reprinting his earlier poem "The Cottage," Turnbull added a new stanza, rebuking aristocratic luxury as plainly as Burns does in "Is there for honest poverty." His satirical poem "The Clubs" gives, however, a more detached or cautious view, portraying the heated political enthusiasm and debate in the Dumfries inns as not so different from other forms of convivial intoxication:

> Another vows his resolution
> Is to o'erturn the constitution.
> A chap, mair noisy than the rest,

---

[6] Roy, *Letters,* II: 256-258.

> Declares he likes the——what is't, best?
> And swears, by blood, and death, and hell—
> He kens what he would do himsel'!
> Whilst others, at a less expence,
> Are counted miracles of sense;
> Important looks, and shrugs, and hitches,
> Do mair than twenty learned speeches!

1794 saw the break-up of Williamson's Dumfries theatre company. Turnbull emigrated to America, joining a theatre company in Charleston, South Carolina in November 1795 and, aside from brief tours, he remained in Charleston the rest of his life. While the immediate reason for emigrating was presumably economic, he also embraced the young republic as a land of political freedom, writing patriotic odes to Columbus and for General Washington's birthday. He lived at then-modest addresses in downtown Charleston; records suggest that the Turnbulls did not have slaves. In May 1796, he wrote a poem about the major fire that swept through Charleston. Following the British-American War of 1812, he took American citizenship.

Charleston had long had Scottish connections, but during the Revolution some prominent Charleston Scots had been loyalists, and Scottishness fell under suspicion. Turnbull still identified himself strongly as a Scot. He brought to the Charleston stage a number of Scottish plays that had been in the Dumfries repertoire, including Home's *Douglas,* Ramsay's *Gentle Shepherd* (for its Charleston premiere), as well as *Oscar and Malvina* and his own comedy *The Recruit.* He went on writing and publishing poetry in the Charleston newspapers and other American periodicals, though his proposal to publish a new collection, in 1796 and again in 1800, came to nothing. In 1808 one of his Scots poems, "The Auld Fiddle," was republished in the prestigious Philadelphia magazine *Port Folio,* perhaps through the interest of another Scottish emigrant poet, Alexander Wilson the ornithologist.

Despite his own truncated formal education, as time went by Turnbull supplemented his work for the theatre by teaching, taking a few students into his house; in the Charleston city directories of 1809 and 1813, his occupation is listed as schoolmaster. Financial security seems to have eluded him. When he died in 1816, aged fifty-one, a Charleston newspaper asked its readers to consider "the melancholy fate of genius crushed by indigence" (*Charleston Courier*, June 3, 1816).

INTRODUCTION

Yet he does not seem to have been discontented. One of the new poems he published in Charleston offered advice to "a friend dissatisfied with his situation" (*Columbia Herald*, May 23, 1796):

> In vain from place to place we roam,
> In vain we quit our native home,
> In vain explore tempestuous seas,
> To purchase happiness and ease.
> And hope to find serener skies
> Where, undisturbed, contentment lies.
> ......
> Bright reason wisely whispers "Care,
> Weak man, will haunt thee ev'rywhere:"
> Content alone can boast the charm
> That can the busy fiend disarm,
> And care will ever fly the cell
> Where innocence and Virtue dwell.

Equally good-humoured is his last poem in Scots, " A Legacy," published in the *Columbian Herald* (March 24, 1796), in the voice of an old schoolmaster settling his modest effects at the end of his life:

> Now, Jook, if I should chance to die,
> And leave my hale estate to thee,
> 'Tis fit that ye should hae a guess
> Of what ye shortly may possess;
> Lest some ane sue ye fur a share,
> You, I appoint the lawfu' heir
> Of a' my siller, goods, and gear ...
> .. what will much delight a scholar,
> Ye'll get an inkglass and a roller,
> A pencase of a spleuchan made,
> A broken knife that wants the blade,
> A pair of specks that want the een,
> Yet better specks were never seen ...
> A psalm book and a bagpipe's drone,
> A mouse trap and a lexicon....

The items bequeathed prove comically worthless, as the testator recognizes, but the tone, the relationship, is itself a legacy.

It is not necessary to make exaggerated claims for Turnbull's Scottish poetry to assert its continuing interest. If Turnbull is still, in his own phrase, "a bard unkend," his poems are worth rediscovery. The poetry of Burns's Ayrshire contemporaries, the poetry written by labouring-class Scottish poets, and the stylistic interplay between 18th century poetry in Scots and that written in the Augustan tradition—all these have been receiving renewed scholarly and critical attention.[7] Beyond or alongside these scholarly concerns, however, Turnbull's poetry retains a human interest, carrying his lively voice across the passing of two centuries.

***

This selection of Gavin Turnbull's Scots poems draws on advance research at the University of South Carolina for the first-ever collected edition of Turnbull's work, which I am co-editing with John Knox and Rachel Mann, in the Centre for Digital Humanities, with additional research assistance from Eric Roper. The initial text entry of Turnbull's poems was by Sej Harman, who was involved for many years in the production of *Studies in Scottish Literature*, and I am grateful to Rachel Mann, Eric Roper, and Joseph DuRant, for proof-reading. The project has been supported by an ASPIRE grant from the university's Vice-President for Research; Eric's participation was partially funded by a South Carolina Honors College Explorer grant. The collected edition will be issued both in open-access digital and print-on-demand formats.

Turnbull, as both a Scottish poet and a South Carolinian, seems an especially appropriate author for the Scottish Poetry Reprints series, an occasional series initiated in 1970 by the late G. Ross Roy. The series is now published in connection with the journal *Studies in Scottish Literature*. In its new format, both print and digital, the series will focus primarily on texts and research from the University of South Carolina's G. Ross Roy Collection.

Patrick Scott

University of South Carolina

---

[7] See, e.g., Carol McGuirk, *Robert Burns & the Sentimental Era* (Athens, GA: University of Georgia P, 1985); David Hill Radcliffe, "Imitation, Popular Literacy and 'The Cotter's Saturday Night'," in *Critical Essays on Robert Burns*, ed. Carol McGuirk (New York: G. K. Hall, 1998), 251-279; Corey E. Andrews, "'Almost the same but not quite': English Poetry by Eighteenth-Century Scots," *Eighteenth Century: Theory and Interpretation*, 47:1 (2006): 59-79; Nigel Leask, *Robert Burns and Pastoral* (Oxford: Oxford UP, 2010); Gerard Carruthers, "Robert Burns's Scots Poetry Contemporaries," in *Burns and Other Poets*, ed. David Sergeant and Fiona Stafford (Edinburgh: Edinburgh UP, 2012): 38-52; Carol McGuirk, *Reading Robert Burns* (London: Pickering & Chatto, 2014), esp. ch. 1; Corey E. Andrews, *The Genius of Scotland* (Amsterdam: Rodopi, 2015), esp. pp. 94-103.

CONTENTS

Introduction	5
To the Scottish Muse	17
The Cottage	17
Sale of Stationary Ware at Buchanan's Head, K*******ck	19
To a Taylor, with Cloth for a New Suit	21
Epistle to a Black-Smith	22
Ode to D**** S*****	24
Elegy on a Curious Original	25
The Auld Fiddle	28
Elegy on a Famous Philosopher	29
Song	31
Prologue to *The Gentle Shepherd*	32
The Clubs: A Satire	34
A Legacy	36
Sources and Notes	39
Selected References	45

POETICAL ESSAYS,

IN THE

SCOTTISH DIALECT.

Divisional or half-title from Gavin Turnbull, *Poetical Essays* (1788), p. [175].

To the Scottish Muse

O come, thou sweetly smiling Maid,
    Wha aft, on Caledonian hills,
With antient Bards delighted stray'd,
    By mossy banks and winding rills;
What time lone philomela fills
    The woodlands with her ev'ning sang,
And shepherd lads, on aiten quills,
    Slow to their cottage piping gang.

Aft hast thou highly deign'd to raise
    The youth in lanely cottage born,
By thee inspir'd, the circling bays,
    The simple Poet's brows adorn.
O tent my pray'r, sweet Maid, nor scorn
    To take me in thy tunefu' train,
Sae shall thy praises, e'en and morn,
    Be sung to ilka hill and plain.

The Cottage

Hail lowly roofs, where pure contentment dwells.

  Within the windings of yon woody dale,
  Beside a burnie, on a bonny green,
  Where raws of whitening hawthorns scent the gale,
  A wee bit canty theicket house is seen;
  Fu' snug it stands frae angry winds, I ween,
  Around, the stacks in rising cones appear,
  Which shaw the owner thrifty is and bien,
  Nae pride has he, nor heaps of worthless geer,
But routh o' kintra fare, the winter days to cheer.

Here stands the barn, to hoord the ripen'd grain,
With lowly roof, of strae and divets made,
Where aft the farmer wheels, with might and main,
The whirling flail, and nae ignoble trade:
And there the milk-house, where the dairy maid
Aft skims the boyns, and presses out the whey;
And here a place, where carts and pleughs are laid;
And there the stable, for the horse and kye;
And here the hen-house stands, and there the grumphies' stye.

Into the ha' house if ye chance to keek,
Ye'll tent the ingle blinkin bonnily,
The crazy rafters, painted o'er wi' reek;
A twa-arm'd chair within the neuk ye'll see,
Where aft the guidman leans, wi' meikle glee,
And smoaks his pipe, and tells his pawky tale,
An antic ambry, made of aiken tree,
Wi' caps and luggies, rang'd upon a dale,
And meikle toop-horn spoons, and plates to haud the kail.

Ben i' the spence, for parlour hae they nane,
The wa's are brawly whiten'd o'er wi' lime;
A polish'd chimla, and a clean hearth-stane;
A keeking-glass, a clock to met the time;
A curtain'd bed, and eke a cupboard prime:
The house contains nae mae fligairy things,
(For luxury is sure an unco crime)
Yet, frae this little wealth, contentment springs,
And thro' the roof, the voice of discord never rings.

Ye, who in lordly halls and bow'rs abide,
And at who's nod obsequious menials bend,
May boast your gay attire and gilded pride,
And rant and roar, and many thousands spend.
But cou'd your haughty minds once condescend
To leave a while the formulas of state,
Ye'd see sweet peace and happiness attend
The humble cot, and at an easy rate,
More real joy and bless the simple swains await.

Selected Poems in the Scottish Dialect 19

Sale of Stationary Ware
at Buchanan's Head, K*******ck

"To a the Warle be it kend,"
That I by Auction do intend
Great routh o' Goods and Geer to vend,
    At lowest price;

Sae, pray good people, all attend
    If ye be wise.

Imprimis, then, I can content ye,
Wi' learned Books, and Bibles plenty,
Gilt on the backs, and bound right dainty,
    In good ca'f sheep:
Glow'r at them weil, and I's indent ye
    Shall buy them cheap.

The rev'rend Brethren o' the band,
May hae whatever they demand,
And, they wha like, I winna stand,
    To sell or niffer;
Bring goods or siller I' yer hand,
    We winna differ,

The Wit and Scholar here may find,
A' that can please a learned mind,
As, Robin Hood, and Captain Hind,
    And other sparks;
But, what leaves a' the rest behind,
    My Father's Warks.[1]

The Book of Knowledge, that can tell
A' things in heav'n, in earth, and hell;
Wi' Hocus Pocus, magic spell,
    For greedy rooks;
To ragged Chapmen too, I sell

---

[1] *Hymns and Spiritual Songs.*

>   Cheap Question Books.
> I've Wax and Wafers, Ink and Quills,
> And best o' Paper frae the mills,
> For bundles, bumfodder or bills,
>   For book or letter,
> There's nane sae good; cheap, cheap it sells,
>   For ready catter.
>
> But what's of a' the rarest show,
> My Pictures, rang'd in seemly row;
> Here twelve good Rules, which we should know;
>   There Captain Bluff;
> Here Peeping Tom, and down below
>   Stands Jamie Duff.[2]
>
> I've China-ware, baith gilt and plain,
> Of which the Ladies are right fain;
> And, to drink punch, or yet champaign,
>   Weil polish'd Glasses;
> And something else, I'll no explain,
>   For bonny Lasses.
>
> I've Heucks, to sheer the harvest corn;
> Good Cudgels, made of varnish'd thorn;
> Rare Spluchangs, ance by sea-dogs worn,
>   And wyllie foxes;
> Braw Sneeshing-mills, o' brass and horn;
>   And Barber's Boxes.
>
> I hae Pomatum for the hair;
> Good plated Buckles, round and square;
> I hae Black-ball, the choicest ware
>   E'er gaed on leather;
> I've Hoops and Rings, and Ribbons rare,
>   And a' thegither.
>
> The chiel that's hardly worth a groat,

---

[2] A natural fool well known in Edinburgh.

May be provided wi' a Coat
At second hand, and no ae jot
   The war o' wear;
And Breeks and Waistcoats may be got,
     And Bonnets here.

I've Whips, and Spurs, and Bits for bridles;
Clear plated Stirrup-Ir'ns for saddles;
Therm-strings for spinning wheels, and fiddles;
   And, may be soon,
I'll have good Pats, and Pans, and Ladles,
     Or a' be done.

To a Taylor
with cloth for a new suit

Braid claith lends fowk an unco heeze,
Makes mony katl-worms butterflies,
Gi'es mony a Doctor his degrees
   For little skaith;
In short ye may be what ye please
     Wi' good braid claith.
                   FERGUSSON

A poet, tatter'd and forlorn,
Whase coat and breeks are sadly torn,
Wha lately sue'd for aid divine,
Now, Taylor, maun apply for thine;
Soliciting thy useful art,
Its needy succour to impart.
Ance manners could compleat a man,
But now the Taylor only can.

   O Taylor, this is true, I ween,
As I've by sad experience seen,
Whatever talents we possess,
Are a' inferior to our dress;
A ragged Bard, however gabby;
Will ay be counted dull and shabby;
And since my coat and breeks turn'd duddy,

I hae been scorn'd by ilka body.
   But trust me, Taylor, soon ye'll see
An unco, sudden change on me;
   My friends will ken me ance again,
      And some what kent na me short syne,
   Will my acquaintance strive to gain,
      And ca' my dullest verses fine.
See here's the claith, come, cut it out,
A remnant maun be sav'd, nae doubt,
Auld Nick can never want his due,
And will get baith the piece and you;
Then ply your nimble han's wi' speed,
Rattle your sheers and wax your thread,
And mak the utmost haste you can,
To rig me out a gentleman:
If you with these demands comply,
Then, Stitch, your name shall never die.

Epistle to a Black-Smith

Dear Sir, if my unnotic'd name,
Not yet proclaim'd by trump of fame,
Has reach'd your lugs, then swith attend,
This essay of a Bard unkend.

   An honest man, lang may he thrive,
(And ilka honest man alive)
As we were wheeling round the bicker,
Tald me that he was unco sicker
A' this braid shire, and other three,
Contain'd na sic a chiel as thee;
That ye, tho' thumpin at the study,
Cou'd mak a verse on ony body,
In nipping, slie, satiric stile,
Wi' teeth as sharp as ony file.

   Bedeen, I gat upo' my shanks,
And gae the carle routh o' thanks,
And sware an aith, e'en b' my sang,

" His metal I shall try e'er lang;
And then I'll tell ye gif the chiel
Be useless ir'n or temper'd steel."

    It shaws I hae but little gumption,
Tho' no way scanty o' presumption,
To bourd wi' ane of sic engine,
And parts sae far exceeding mine;
For, a' that ken ye can declare,
Your match is scarce in ony where,
But my impatience may excuse me,
Lest ye should for a dult abuse me.

    O wad my scanty purse but spare,
That I might tak a jaunt to Ayr,
Ae night wi' thee to sing and roar,
And set auld care ahint the door;
Then we shou'd hae a merry bout,
And no sit dumb nor yet cast out.

    But, lest that we shou'd ne'er forgether,
To get a crack wi' ane anither,
My earnest prayer ay shall be,
For routh o' coals, and ir'n to thee;
That ye may lang be hale and canty,
And ding that cursed carle *want ay*;
That ye may ne'er be scant o' brass,
To synd the spark that's i' yer hause;
That, as ye blaw your smithy fire,
Apollo may your wit inspire,
To gar your easy flowing rhyme,
Just like alternate hammers chime;
And, that your mind be ne'er perplex'd,
But firm as ony anvil fix'd;
That, as your gauds of ir'n ye bow,
Your enemies may yield to you;
May, by the fatal sisters three,
Thy chain of life extended be,
Till unto langest life thy dust,
Stand proof against the teeth of rust;

And, when grim Death, wi' fatal dart,
Shall gar thy saul and body part,
May this thy Epitaph be made,
"Here Vulcan lies, a matchless Blade."

Ode to D**** S*****

By this ye'll figure to yoursel'
Dear lad, the method how I dwell,
    And pass the lanely time:
In a wee housie, warm and snug,
I sit beside the chimla lug,
    And spin awa my rhyme.
Sometimes the weary ploy I curse,
    That fortune to my share
Has thrawn, which ever hauds my purse
    Sae toom, and back sae bare:
        Then grumbling, and mumbling,
          I thraw awa my pen
        For ever mair, never
          To write for tasteless men.

The greatest dults that ever wrote,
Have often Noble Patrons got,
    Their nonsense to protect;
Whilst chiels of maist ingine and skill,
Unnotic'd, unrewarded still,
    Meet nought but cauld neglect.
O Pæn's[3] sons, how I repine
    At your unhappy lot,
While empty naethings glare and shine,
    Your mem'ries are forgot.
        Yet time will sublime still
          A' true poetic lays;
        And glorious, victorious,
          Bestow the weil earn'd bays.

---

[3] Apollo.

Then heed na, Davie, tho' we be
A race expos'd to misery,
    A' mankind hae their skair;
Yet, wi' the few whase hearts are fir'd
Wi' love o' sang, by Him inspir'd,
    What mortals can compare:
How sweet, when in the feeling heart,
    Alternate passions glow,
The mix'd ideas to impart,
    To paint our joy and wo;
        Desire conspires
            Wi' love, to form the sang,
        While pleasing, and easing,
            The numbers glide alang.

The sweets of nature a' are ours,
The verdant fields, the blooming flow'rs,
    The woodland and the plain:
To us the bonny months of spring,
Delights and saft sensations bring,
    The vulgar ne'er attain.
How sweet, when night is calm and still,
    Beneath pale Phœbe's ray,
Alang the margin of a rill,
    To wind our lanely way;
        Still musing, and chusing,
            Ideas fit to move
        Some charmer, and warm her,
            With all the flames of love.

Elegy on a Curious Original

I sing the man of wondrous skill,
The best that ever blew a quill,
Or keepit gimmers, on a hill
    By Tay or Tweed,
Or Irvine water, smooth and still,
    Wha now is dead.

Ay when he play'd, the sheep advanc'd,
The yowes and lams thegither danc'd,
The awkward cattle lap and pranc'd,
    Wi' clumsy speed;
And lightfoot look'd like ane entranc'd,
    To hear his reed.

The lasses gather'd him about,
And ilka gaping kintra lout
Led on the dance, an unco rout,
    And through the reel,
They toss'd the hizzies, in and out,
    And gart them squeel.

He fidg'd, and leugh, to see the fun,
Cry'd, till't again, I'm scarce begun;
He wha a bonny lass wad won,
    Maun wallup here,
Then up he play'd the cutty-gun,
    Their hearts to cheer.

What signifies a piper's drone,
Or fiddle, for to play upon,
'Bout ilka smooth Italian tone
    Mak nae mair bustle,
Willie cou'd gar them a' stan' yon'
    Just wi' a whistle.

Beside his elbow stood a bicker,
For he made ay his mouthfu' sicker,
And for to mak him play the quicker,
    They fill'd his cap;
He leugh and toutit up the liquor
    Out ilka drap.

This rais'd him to a canty key,
And gart his whistle sound wi' glee;
An unco merry bod was he,
    When ance turn'd sou,

And nane wi' better grace cou'd prie,
    A lasses' mou'.

He had right mony a pawky tale,
To tell outo'er a capfu' ale;
His canty jokes cou'd never fail,
    In time o' need,
To cheer the heart, be't sick or hale,
    But now he's dead.

He had an unco head o' wit,
Was never noddle sure like it;
He was for Priest or Doctor fit,
    And weil did ken a'
The Latin Grammar, ilka bit,
    As far as *Penna*.

He faught, but sinile met wi' scars,
For they were only wordy wars;
He kent the order o' the stars,
    And eke the moon,
Cou'd tell, in Venus, or in Mars,
    Whate'er was done.

Not Ramsey, nor the canty Chiel,
Wha sang Hab Simson's life sae weil,
Nor yet the Bard o' Gilbert fiel',
    Nor Sawny Pope,
Cou'd faster up Parnassus speel,
    To reach the top.

Of a' sic qualities as thae,
He was possess'd, and mony mae,
The neebours said that he cou'd spae,
    And fortunes tell;
I doubt it, but if it was sae,
    He kent himsel'.

The Auld Fiddle
a poem occasioned
by a person's treading on it
and crushing it to pieces

We see that each revolving day,
The rarest earthly things decay;
Nor can our best inventions save
Them frae the universal grave:
Still some disaster, unforeseen,
Maks them as they had never been.

   See my auld Fiddle, ance sae good,
Which pat me aft in merry mood
When a' things fail'd; see, in disguise,
In broken fragments where she lies,
Thrawn in a neuk wi' ither lumber,
Nae mair my study to encumber;
Of brig and finger-brod bereft,
Nae string, nor bass, nor tenor left;
Her hand broke aff, her wame shot in,
And for to tune her ne'er a pin;
Her back and sides in waefu' case,
Sad monuments of her disgrace.

   Nae mair, alas! on her I'll play
Piano sweet, or blithe Strathspey;
Nae mair, when dowie thoughts invade,
Shall she be summon'd to my aid:
Like some auld trophy she may hing,
A dismal melancholy thing.

   What tho' she was of beauteous frame,
And frae the far Cremona came,
Yet that, and a' her tones sae sweet,
Cou'd not award the murd'rer's feet,
Wha, heedless what he heard or saw,
Crush'd her poor banes against the wa';
A mournfu' echo, sad and sweet,
Resounded wi' his clumsy feet:

Sae Poets tell before she die,
The swan sings her own elegy.

    May minstrels a' the villain hate,
And mock and jeer him air and late;
May his dull lugs be ever found,
Deaf to the harmony of sound;
May discord deave him night and day,
And corbies sing his fun'ral lay;
While my auld Fiddle, tho's she's lame,
Is sounded by the voice of fame.

    Ye wand'ring spirits of the wind,
May ye my silent Fiddle find,
And, as ye tak your nightly rounds,
Recal, as erst, enchanting sounds.
Methinks I hear M'Pherson there,
Awake some Caledonian air,
Or Handel, master o' the band,
Employ his sound-compelling hand:
Haste, haste, ye tunefu' shapes of air,
And to my ruin'd strings repair.

Elegy
on a Famous Philosopher

Nae mair I'll greet and mak a main,
For chiels that's neither dead nor gane,
But wail, in doolfu' dumps, for ane
    Of wondrous meed,
For death, a worthy wight has tane,
    J*** G*****'s dead.

Thou'rt ever an unwelcome guest,
A waefu' horror breathing pest,
As weil's the worst the vera best,
    Can naething plead;
A famous man by a' confest,
    J*** G*****'s dead.

Ye tyrant pow'r, ye dinna care,
The man o' parts and knowledge rare,
Ye'll nane, for a' their wisdom spare,
    Without remeed,
The vera heart and saul o' lair,
    J*** G*****'s dead.

Ye might far better tane awa
Some body guid for nought ava,
Sae looten a' your vengeance fa'
    On some weak head,
And no gien sic a man a ca'
    As him that's dead.

I trow ye little kent his merit,
What wondrous gifts he did inherit;
He had a clear enlightening spirit,
    A shining glead,
But a' that's guid is wi' him carrit,
    For now he's dead.

Auld Killie, mourn in sable hue,
The sad and dreary day ye'll rue,
Wha'll open nature to your view,
    And wisdom spread?
Sic men as G***** were but few,
    And now he's dead.

Wha will explain the circling year,
And represent the rolling Sphere;
Or make the Solar System clear,
    As ony bead,
J*** G***** cou'd, what need ye speer?
    But now he's dead.

Tho' he gat little o' the school,
He'd prove, by an unerring rule,
That Newton was a frantic fool,
    A crazy head;

And soon had bred him muckle dool,
　　But now he's dead.

He play'd an unco manfu' part,
And had the Gospel-cause at heart,
Recover'd it, wi' toil and smart;
　　A doughty deed,
And pure Religion did revert,
　　But now he's dead.

As mony a man has heard him tell,
He hated bigotry like hell,
Yet had a System, by himsel',
　　Which was his Creed,
Frae modern wits he bore the bell,
　　But now he's dead.

He was a man without a flaw,
In's life he never err'd at a',
His ain opinion was the law,
　　Withouten feed;
The world to him were madmen a',
　　But now he's dead.

His Epitaph

Here lies a man without a match,
Ne'er ane did sic strange fancies hatch;
Of a' the men, sin' Adam fell,
No ane was right yet but himsel'.

Song

Tune: *The mucking o' Geordie's byre.*

Ye lads that are plaguet wi' lasses,
　　Had need to be tenty and slie,
Or soon ye'll be guidet like asses,
　　Gif ye be as silly as me.
I courted a lassie for siller,

And she was right saucy and sprie;
But 'gin I was buckl'd until her,
   The fient a scrap siller had she.

But kent ye the way how I gat her,
   Ye'd say it was cunning o' me;
The chiels a' gaed wood to be at her,
   Sae cadgie the siller to see:
But I gied her something to carry,
   A sure memorandum to be,
And syne she consentet to marry,
   And wad hae nae ither but me.

In a doop she began to grow wally,
   The neebours a' fairli't to see;
But I kent the reason fu' brawly,
   Wha soon was a daddy to be.
And when the black cutty we mountet,
   Her lads a' leugh hearty at me;
But O how my courage was bluntet,
   When fient a scrap siller had she.

Prologue to
The Gentle Shepherd

Sirs, I'm a Ghaist!—but dinna fear me,
I'm Ramsay's Ghaist!—ay, now ye'll hear me;—
Frae sweet Elysium's bonny bow'rs,
Where Poets pass their blissfu' hours,
I come, and dinna scorn to tell,
Only to justify mysel'.

   When Death, that camsheugh carl, had fell'd me,
And first Elysian fouk beheld me,
My auld blue bonnet on my head,
And hamely Caledonian weed;
They cry'd, "preserve's: what's yon droll body,
That gangs just like a niddy noddy?
'Tis some bit poor auld Scottish herd":

Selected Poems in the Scottish Dialect

"Na faith!" quo' Hermes, "he's a Bard,
Sic as the deel a' mae ye'll find,
And ane of the Dramatic kind."
Syne he pronounc'd aloud my name,
A current passport for my fame.

Then I shook hands wi' Johny Dryden,
And twa-three mae, wham much we pride in;
As Irish Ben[4], and Warwick Willy[5],
Wha's, by my saul, a matchless Billy;
And poor Tam Oatway, wha' could blaw
The sweetest whistle of them a'!
And a' that had a spunk of grace
Gied me kind welcome to the place;
But ane, wha look'd as if I stunk,
The chiel was either daft or drunk,
And though he had but little gumption,
'Twas mair than balanc'd by presumption;
Said, in a kind of leering way,
"Friend! sure ye never read a play;
Or if ye had, 'tis plain enough,
Ye ne'er could fancy sic damn'd stuff,
As Scottish Shepherds' uncouth rhyms,
Could grace the stage and please the times".

Guidman, quoth I, whate'er's your name
I dinna ken, but never blame
Things as far past your comprehension,
As is the very Piece ye mention;
And though ye may think little o't,
I'll wager you a sterling groat,
Or, what a Poet values mair,
This wreath that I hae round my hair,
Against that wither'd twig of thine,
I'll get applause for ilka line!

Now, Sirs, I sweat wi' very fright,

---

[4] *Ben Johnston*
[5] *Shakespear*

Lest ye should hiss my play this night;
For Actors are grown sae refin'd,
They never speak it to my mind;
Sae if the Piece its beauty tine,
Ye canna say the wyte was mine:
Yet, O! be sparing for my sake,
For if ye hiss, I lose my *stake*!

The Clubs
A Satire

Now, jowing bells, with solemn croon,
Proclaim another day is done,
And fowk wha due decorum keep,
Forget their cares in silent sleep ;
While jovial sauls that fear nae ill,
Keep up the noise and riot still.
Loud rings the tavern but and ben,
With men turn'd sots, and sots turn'd men.
Here, may we see a drunken core,
That can do nought but sing and roar ;
Ane, ocean fu' of nappy liquor,
Lilts at auld Moses and the Vicar ;
A fat guidman, at the board head,
Laments John Barlycorn is dead ;
Ane, the maist jovial of the quorum,
Cries " damn ye ! gie me Tullochgorum."
And here, a Counsellor, hum drum,
Sits sweetly tuning " ti, ta, tum !"
Tam, wi' the bottom of a cap
Comes o'er his nose a cursed rap ;
A Bully, snoring at his side,
Starts up and swers he'll skelp his hide ;
Out o'er he reels, and in his fa',
Breaks table, glasses, bowls an' a'!

Another room a group contains
Of busy, cloud'environ'd brains ;
A set of Politicians, who

Direct the course of things below:
All Europe's fate depends on them,
Baith Indies their attention claim.
Poor Louis' cause is fairly try'd,
With warm debates on either side.
There twa, whas brows portend a storm,
Sit busy planning a reform.
Here ane, his Liege's firmest friend,
Swears he'll the government defend.
Another, vows his resolution
Is, to o'erturn the constitution.
A chap, mair noisy than the rest,
Declares he likes the——what is't, best?
And swears, by blood, and death, and hell—
He kens what he would do himsel'!
Whilst others, at a less expence,
Are counted miracles of sense ;
Important looks, and shrugs, and hitches,
Do mair than twenty learned speeches !

    Let those, my friends, delight in noise,
Incapable for social joys;
Let these 'bout politics debate,
And regulate both *kirk* and *stat* :
With us let all disputes be ended;
The times by words will ne'er be mended.
My principle, if I dare mention ;—
I'm sworn a foe to the Convention.
I'll honour Freedom while I live,
But, such as *British* laws can give!
And though not able to defend
My Liege, my aid I'd freely lend :
And while I've breath I'll gladly sing
That loyal song, " GOD SAVE THE KING !"

A Legacy

Now, Jook, if I should chance to die,
And leave my hale estate to thee,
'Tis fit that ye should hae a guess
Of what ye shortly may possess ;
Lest some ane sue ye for a share,
You, I appoint the lawfu' heir
Of a' my silver, goods and gear,
The inventory follows here.

Imprimis—May I lose my noddle,
If I'm possessed of, e'er a bodle
In a' the world, save, halfpence three,
That Jock the student oweth me ;
Get it from him by hook or crook.
He ow'st me for a Latin book.
But what will much delight a scholar,
Ye'll get a ink glass, and a roller,
A pen case of a splu has made,
A broken knife, that wants the blade,
A pair of specks that want the een,
Yet better specks were never seen:
And likewise, laddie, ye will get
The frame that ance was round a slate,
A cane that's broken by the middle
The brig and belly of a fiddle
A psalm book, and a bagpipe's drone,
A mouse trap, and a lexicon ;
And what's of greater value still,
The lid of my auld sneeshing mill!

Ye'll get a Hat that once was new,
Though now it's neither black nor blue,
But just between a grey and brown,
Japann'd wi' creesh about the crown ;
Item, a glove of ramskin leather,
That coor'd my hands in frosty weather,
A Purse made of a mouse's skin,

I held, when rich, my silver in—
But hoolie—I had maist neglected
To mention ae thing, much respected—
I mean a Boiler, made of tin,
Runs as fast out as ye'll fill in :
Such was, as ancient Poets tell,
The lecky bottom'd Tub of hell—
A rusty lock, a three-leg'd stool,
And ae lith of a twa-foot rule,
Twa chair, of great antiquity,
Ten times the age of thee or me;
The tane, indeed, no unco stout,
For aft the bottom tumbles out,
Which gies me mony a weary coup,
And lands me backward on my doup;
On this mysel' I sometimes lean,
I keep the other for a friend.

   If I had any mair to gie,
Nae other man my heir should be:
Sae guide it weel, and I'll indent ye
Shall never want, while ye hae plenty.

SOURCES AND NOTES

To the Scottish Muse (p. 17): first published in *Poetical Essays* (1788), 177.
 p. 17: *tent:* heed

The Cottage (p. 17): first published in *Poetical Essays*, (1788), 178-180; revised, with an additional stanza, for *Poems* (1794), 17-19; reprinted in *Columbian Herald and New Daily Advertiser* [Charleston, SC] (March 8, 1796). Radcliffe suggests that this poem's treatment of rural life is in the tradition of Shenstone's *The Schoolmistress*, but it also alludes more generally to Robert Fergusson, "The Farmer's Ingle," and Robert Burns, "The Cottar's Saturday Night."
Epigraph: unattributed. Cf. "Where hermit peace with mild contentment dwells": William Julius Mickle, *Liberty: An Elegy to the Memory of his Royal Highness Frederic, late Prince of Wales*, line 48 [*English Poetry Database* from Mickle, *Poetical Works* (1806)]; and "And rural huts, where sweet contentment dwells": Edward Ward, *Honesty in Distress, but reliev'd by no Party*, Act 1, line 2 [*English Poetry Database*, from Ward, *Miscellaneous Writings*, III (1712)].
 p. 17: *bien:* comfortable
 routh: plenty.
 p. 18: *boyns:* the milk-pan.
 grumphies: pigs. In 1788, this line read: "And here the hen-house stands, and there the stinking stye."
 ambry: cupboard.
 keeking-glass: looking-glass, mirror.
 Ye, who in lordly halls: this stanza was added in 1794.

Sale of Stationary Ware at Buchanan's Head, K*****ck** (p. 19): first published in *Poetical Essays* (1788), 181-185. The footnotes to the text are Turnbull's. Paterson comments that "Who the 'man of all wares'

... was, we have not ascertained, nor can our friends in Kilmarnock remember any house or shop having the sign of 'Buchanan's Head'" (Paterson, *Contemporaries of Burns*, 109). The shop-sign presumably featured a portrait of the learned Renaissance Scottish neo-Latin poet George Buchanan (1506-1583). In the 1720s and 1730s, "Buchanan's Head" had been the shop-sign (and imprint) for the London shop of two Scottish bookseller, James McEuen, and his more famous successor Andrew Millar, publisher of James Thomson.

p. 19: *niffer:* swap or barter.
My Father's Warks: Turnbull's footnote, *Hymns and Spiritual Songs,* may refer to the collections by Isaac Watts (1707-1709, but frequently reprinted) or by John and Charles Wesley (1753), or perhaps even to a local collection of this title recently printed by Turnbull's own publisher David Niven for a congregation in Grammar-School Wynd, Glasgow.

p. 20: *catter:* cash.
Jamie Duff: the picture (engraving) that the Kilmarnock bookshop was offering for sale was one of John Kay's Edinburgh portraits. Jamie (or "Baillie") Duff, who died in 1788, was a well-known Edinburgh eccentric who joined in local funeral processions, dressed in mourning, later adding a cheap gilt chain and awarding himself the title of Baillie: see James Paterson and James Maidment, *Kay's Edinburgh Portraits,* 2 vols. (London: Hamilton, Adams; Glasgow: Morison, 1885), I: 18-20.
Heucks: sickles, or perhaps scythes.
Spluchangs: tobacco-pouches.
Sneeshing-mills: snuff boxes (sneezing mulls).

p. 21: *Therm-strings:* thairm or catgut cord.

To a Taylor with Cloth for a New Suit (p. 21): first published in *Poetical Essays* (1788), 186-187.
Epigraph: Robert Fergusson, "Braid Claith," lines 43-48, in *Poems of Robert Fergusson*, ed. Matthew P. MacDiarmid (Edinburgh: Scottish Text Society, 1954-1956), vol. II, p. 81.

Epistle to a Black-Smith (p. 22): first published in *Poetical Essays* (1788), 188-190. The addressee of this poem, an unidentified blacksmith-poet in Ayr, is not the same as the "William Reid, Blacksmith," for whose comedy *The Heroine,* performed in Dumfries, Turnbull would write a theatrical prologue, which he later published in the *Columbian Herald and New Daily Advertiser* [Charleston, SC] (March 26, 1796).

p. 22: *swith:* rapidly, quickly.

SOURCES AND NOTES

Ode to D** S***** (p. 24): first published in *Poetical Essays* (1788), 191-193. The Ayrshire poet David Sillar (1760-1830) was a friend of Burns and fellow-member of the Tarbolton Bachelors' Club. Burns wrote two verse-epistles to Sillar, one first published in Sillar's own collection, *Poems* (Kilmarnock: John Wilson, 1789); see *Poems and Songs*, ed. Kinsley, 3 vols. (Oxford: Clarendon, 1969), I: 65, 240. Paterson notes that Turnbull's Ode, "both in versification and sentiment, is an imitation of Burns's 'First Epistle to Davie,' and we should think not greatly inferior in merit" (Paterson, *Contemporaries of Burns*, 95).
p. 25: *a mankind ha' their skair:* all men have their share [of troubles].

Elegy on a Curious Original (p. 25): first published in *Poetical Essays* (1788), 197-201.
p. 27: *Ramsey:* Allan Ramsay (1686-1758), the Scottish poet for whose play *The Gentle Shepherd* Turnbull wrote a prologue.
the canty chiel: Robert Sempill (1596-1663), whose "Lament for Habbie Simpson" was the first poem in the "Standard Habbie" metre later used by both Robert Fergusson and Burns.
the Bard o' Gilbert fiel': William Hamilton of Gilbertfield (1665-1751), who wrote a modern verse life of William Wallace.
Sawny Pope: the poet Alexander Pope (1688-1744), notable for the ease with which he claimed to write when young: "I lisp'd in numbers."
speel: clamber, climb.

The Auld Fiddle (p. 28): first published in *Poetical Essays*, (1788), 202-204; reprinted as "Elegy on My Auld Fiddle," *Port Folio* [Philadelphia], 6 (August 20, 1808): 127-128. *The Port Folio*, one of the more prestigious American magazines of the period, was published by Bradford and Inskeep, for whom the Scottish poet and ornithologist Alexander Wilson worked as an editor from 1806 till 1813. Earlier, in 1807, the same magazine had published another Turnbull poem, "Ode to Suspicion."
p. 29: *M'Pherson:* perhaps James MacPherson (1675-1700), for whom the fiddle tune "MacPherson's Rant" is named, who before his execution as an outlaw was reputed to have broken his own fiddle on the scaffold.

Elegy on a Famous Philosopher (p. 29): published in *Poetical Essays*, (1788), 209-212. John Goldie (1717-1811), a cabinet-maker and then wine-merchant in Kilmarnock, was a notable local controversialist, putting forward progressive religious ideas in opposition to Auld Licht traditionalism. His books included *Essays on Various Important*

Subjects, Moral and Divine (3 vols., 180), and *The Gospel Recovered from Its Captive State* (1786). Burns had written a verse-epistle to John Goldie in 1785 (*Poems and Songs*, ed. Kinsley, 3 vols. [Oxford: Clarendon, 1969], II: 114-115), and Goldie was one of those who encouraged Burns to publish *Poems, Chiefly in the Scottish Dialect* (Kilmarnock: Wilson, 1786).

p. 30: *Auld Killie:* perhaps a generic reference to the inhabitants of Kilmarnock, or more specifically the members of Kilmarnock Kilwinning Lodge, for whom Burns wrote the song "The Sons of old Killie" (Kinsley I: 299; written 1786 but not published till 1834).

p. 31: *withouten feed:* i.e. without [a lawyer] being paid.

Song: "Ye lads that are plaguet wi' lasses" (p. 31): first published as a separate song in *Poetical Essays*, (1788), 178-180; reprinted as the first song in Turnbull's comedy *The Recruit*, in *Poems* (1794), 38-39; and again with the songs from *The Recruit* in *Columbian Herald and New Daily Advertiser* [Charleston, SC] (February 19, 1796). The air Turnbull used, "The Muckin' o' Geordie's Byre," had appeared in *Orpheus Caledonius* (1733), no. 33; *Caledonian Pocket Companion*, II (1745), 35; and (with earlier words) in Johnson, *Scots Musical Museum*, I (1787), no. 96; it was also used later by Burns for his song "Adown winding Nith I did wander" (Kinsley II:701), published in Thomson, *Select Collection of Original Scotish Airs*, II: set 3 (1799), song 66. *The Recruit* was first performed for Turnbull's benefit performance in Dumfries in January, 1794. It was staged at the City Theatre, Church Street, Charleston, again for Turnbull's benefit night, on March 11, 1796, and again at the Charleston Theatre, Broad Street, Charleston, on May 30, 1807.

p. 31: *tenty:* attentive.

Prologue to *The Gentle Shepherd* (p. 32): first published *Poems* (1794), 10-12; reprinted in *Columbian Herald and New Daily Advertiser* [Charleston, SC] (March 11, 1796). The footnotes to the text are Turnbull's. Allan Ramsay's pastoral comedy *The Gentle Shepherd* was a staple of late eighteenth-century Scottish theatre; Turnbull's prologue was written for the Dumfries Theatre. While the play was well-known to American readers, it had never been staged in Charleston before the performance at the City Theatre, on April 30, 1796, "under the Sanction and Patronage of the R.W. Grand Lodge of South Carolina Ancient York Masons," when Turnbull played Bauldy and his wife played Mause.

p. 34: *tine:* lose.

SOURCES AND NOTES

The Clubs: A Satire (p. 34): first published in *Poems* (1794), 10-12; reprinted in *Columbian Herald and New Daily Advertiser* [Charleston, SC] (March 15, 1796). Robert Crawford has recently contrasted Turnbull's conclusion here that he will "gladly sing / That loyal song 'GOD SAVE THE KING!,'" with the political ambiguity of Burns's conclusion to his song "The Dumfries Volunteers, that "While we sing God save the King, / We'll ne'er forget the People!" (Crawford, *The Bard* [Princeton: Princeton University Press, 2009], 385; *Poems and Songs*, ed. Kinsley, 3 vols. (Oxford: Clarendon, 1969), II: 764-765, III: 1469). In December 1792, a riot had broken out in the Dumfries Theatre when radicals in the audience called for singing the French revolutionary song "Ça ira," while hissing "God save the King": see *Letters of Robert Burns*, ed. G. Ross Roy, 2 vols. (Oxford: Clarendon, 1985), II: 166, 173.

A Legacy (p. 36): first published in *Columbian Herald and New Daily Advertiser* [Charleston, SC] (March 24, 1796). Though Turnbull's formal schooling had been cut short, during his later years in Charleston, he supplemented his work for the stage with teaching, and he is listed as "schoolmaster" in the Charleston City Directories for 1809 and 1813.
p. 36: *splu:* tobacco-pouch.
sneeshing mill: snuff box (sneezing mull).

SELECTED REFERENCES

Andrews, Corey E., "'Almost the same but not quite': English Poetry by Eighteenth-Century Scots," *Eighteenth Century: Theory and Interpretation*, 47:1 (2006): 59-79.

_____, "'Far-Fam'd RAB': Scottish Labouring-Class Poets Writing in the Shadow of Robert Burns, 1785-1792," *Studies in Hogg and His World* 23 (2013): 41-67.

_____, *The Genius of Scotland: the Cultural Production of Robert Burns, 1785-1834* (Amsterdam: Rodopi, 2015).

Carruthers, Gerard, "Robert Burns's Scots Poetry Contemporaries," in *Burns and Other Poets*, ed. David Sergeant and Fiona Stafford (Edinburgh: Edinburgh UP, 2012): 38-52.

Crawford, Robert, *The Bard: Robert Burns, A Biography* (Princeton: Princeton University Press, 2009).

[Crichton, Thomas], account of Turnbull in his "Biographical Sketches of Alexander Wilson," in *The Weaver* [Paisley], 2 (1819); extract reprinted in Paterson, Appendix, pp. 23-24.

Hook, Andrew, *Scotland and America: A Study of Cultural Relations, 1750-1835*, new ed. (Glasgow: Humming Earth, 2008)

Hagy, James W., *City Directories for Charleston, South Carolina for ... 1803-1813* (Baltimore: Clearful, 1995).

Holcomb, Brent, *South Carolina Naturalizations* (Baltimore: Genealogical Publishing, 1985).

Hoole, W. Stanley, *The Ante-Bellum Charleston Theatre* (Tuscaloosa: Univ. of Alabama Press, 1946).

Kinsley, James, ed., *Poems and Songs of Robert Burns,* 3 vols. (Oxford: Clarendon Press, 1969).

Leask, Nigel, *Robert Burns and Pastoral: Poetry and Improvement in Late Eighteenth-Century Scotland* (Oxford: Oxford University Press, 2010).

McGuirk, Carol, *Robert Burns and the Sentimental Era* (Athens, GA: University of Georgia Press, 1985).
_____, *Reading Robert Burns: Texts, Contexts, Transformations* (London: Pickering & Chatto, 2014).
Paterson, James, *The Contemporaries of Burns, and More Recent Poets of Ayrshire* (Edinburgh: Paton, 1840).
Radcliffe, David Hill, "Imitation, Popular Literacy and 'The Cotter's Saturday Night'," in *Critical Essays on Robert Burns*, ed. Carol McGuirk (New York: G. K. Hall, 1998), 251-279.
_____, "Gavin Turnbull, 1770 ca.-1816," in *Spenser and the Tradition; English Poetry 1579-1830* [1994-], on line at: http://spenserians.cath.vt.edu/AuthorRecord.php?&action=GET&recordid=33336&page=AuthorRecord.
_____, "Turnbull, Gavin (c. 1765-1816)," *Oxford Dictionary of National Biography*, ed. H. C. G. Matthew and Brian Harrison (Oxford: Oxford UP, 2004), 55: 587; updated version at: http://www.oxforddnb.com.pallas2.tcl.sc.edu/view/article/64791?docPos=7.
Rogers, George C., Jr., *Charleston in the Age of the Pinckneys* (Columbia: Univ. of South Carolina Press, 1980).
Roy, G. Ross Roy, ed., *The Letters of Robert Burns*, 2 vols. (Oxford: Clarendon Press, 1985).
Scott, Patrick, "Whatever Happened to Gavin Turnbull? Hunting Down a Friend of Burns in South Carolina," *Robert Burns Lives!*, 159 (November 28, 2012), at: http://www.electricscotland.com/familytree/frank/burns_lives159.htm
_____, "The First Publication of 'Holy Willie's Prayer,'" *Scottish Literary Review*, 7:1 (Spring-Summer, 2015): 1-18.
Sodders, Richard P., *The Theatre Management of Alexandre Placide in Charleston, 1794-1812*, 2 vols., unpub. Ph.D. diss. (Louisiana State University, 1983).
Turnbull, Gavin, *Poetical Essays* (Glasgow: David Niven, 1788).
_____, *Poems* (Dumfries: for the Author, 1794).
Willis, Eola, *The Charleston Stage in the XVIII Century with Social Settings of the Time* (New York: Blum, 1968).

Made in the USA
Charleston, SC
21 June 2015